COOKING
with Clara

COOKING
with Clara

●●●●●●●●●●●●●●●●

Recipes of a Lifetime

Clara Lizio Melchiorre
with Rosie Amodio

Photos by Valentina Sokolova, Art of Vivid

Skyhorse Publishing

Skyhorse Publishing books may be purchased in bulk at special discounts for sales promotion, corporate gifts, fund-raising, or educational purposes. Special editions can also be created to specifications. For details, contact the Special Sales Department, Skyhorse Publishing, 307 West 36th Street, 11th Floor, New York, NY 10018 or info@skyhorsepublishing.com.

Skyhorse® and Skyhorse Publishing® are registered trademarks of Skyhorse Publishing, Inc.®, a Delaware corporation.

Visit our website at www.skyhorsepublishing.com.

10 9 8 7 6 5 4

Library of Congress Cataloging-in-Publication Data is available on file.

Cover photos by Valentina Sokolova and the Melchiorre family

Print ISBN: 978-1-5107-6601-3
Ebook ISBN: 978-1-5107-6602-0

Printed in Canada

CONTENTS

PREFACE

An Italian in the Kitchen

IT'S HARD TO FIND SOMEONE who doesn't like Italian food. And this book makes it easy for you to create Italian food at home. We can thank Clara Lizio Melchiorre, the author of this book, for that.

Clara's story spans four generations. She spent much of her life in the shadow of her famous mom, Mama Celeste Lizio of frozen pizza fame. With her charming Italian-tinged English and "abbondanza" slogan, Clara's mother took over the frozen pizza market in the '70s and '80s—and Clara helped build the business for decades. Then Clara came into her own in the late '80s when she opened her namesake restaurant in a Chicago suburb. Now, as the matriarch of a loving, passionate Italian-American family, Clara is ready to share her cooking techniques and secret recipes with the world.

That's me as a child dressed up as a nun for a big holiday.

This is a promotional shot from a series of videos I made with my daughter, Michelle, in the 1980s.

Clara has always been a powerful personality. Here's how one newspaper article described Clara as a child: "Old-timers remember her as a skinny kid with copper pigtails who did her homework at the bar and demanded that anyone who swore in her presence say Hail Marys in penance." Clara doesn't do that anymore, but she did reference at least three saints during our interviews for this book.

This self-taught chef loves to follow chef-like standards of procedure. Her favorite term is *mise en place*, which is the culinary expression for "better get all your ingredients in order *before* cooking." She's very committed to her procedure, and once you try out a few of her recipes, you will be, too.

"Clara's love for life is expressed in her cooking. She wants to share what she knows and enjoys, and gets gratification out of pleasing everyone around her," says longtime patron and former CEO of Wilton Industries, Vince Naccarato. "Clara is very talented and cooks some of the best homemade food—with love in every bite—that you will ever eat."

Clara redefined the notion of Italian-American cooking. It's not just about throwing together some garlic and olive oil and covering it in mozzarella. Each of her dishes has a special touch or innovation.

Clara never stops perfecting her recipes. She never stops, period. She's a feminist at heart. She's strong—having beaten a rare form of cancer, recovering from an infection that took most of her hearing, and coming back from financial adversity. She's compassionate. She's a food traditionalist who adapts to changing tastes and times—she has gluten-free and nut-free versions of her dishes.

To quote this dynamic woman about cooking, "It's in the family. Before me, after me." And hopefully this book will capture her essence, creativity, and love of cooking.

My daughter, Michelle, with her brothers, Anthony and Rudy,
and our dog, Max, circa 1970.

That's me when I was young.   *My parents serving wedding breakfast at Celeste's for my brother Pat.*

*The children celebrating with Gramma Elsie.
(No Mark yet!)*

*That's me getting a little beer at the
family tavern.*

INTRODUCTION

"Anything made with love is perfect."

—Clara Lizio Melchiorre

I'M 82, I HAVE FOUR CHILDREN, 11 grandchildren and one great-grandchild, a famous mom (she started Mama Celeste frozen pizza), and one namesake restaurant. I've been cooking for four generations. Cooking is my life, and it's taken me all these years to finally write down all I've learned. I have wanted to archive my recipes and tell our family's story for as long as I can remember. With some encouragement from my children and grandchildren, I am finally doing it.

Basically, I really want this collection to be more of a storybook with recipes. A blend of the values my brothers and I grew up with, a special heritage instilled in us by our parents. From humble beginnings, Celeste and Anthony, my mom and dad, gave us a great legacy. I wanted my family to have this written history that celebrates Mom and Dad's love of cooking for generations to come. In our family, we show love through food.

For you, I want to give you very simple and very easy recipes for the novice or seasoned cook. This is a very approachable cookbook. I will walk you through the flavors and techniques and tell you what to do and how to do it. For me, procedure is the most important part of any dish.

It's not too difficult or overwhelming to achieve a very successful dinner from simple foods. To be truthful, I have never had formal cooking lessons but helped run a pasta empire, became chef of my own restaurant, won a few awards, and have been on TV! If I can do it, so can you. My secret? Make things you love, want to share, and pass on.

My love of cooking—food, really—began as a child, growing up on Chicago's West Side. My parents, who emigrated from Sant'Angelo all'Esca, near Naples, opened a grocery store that became known more for what my mom made with the groceries in the tiny back kitchen than for selling the actual ingredients. The smell of her cooking drew WPA workers, whom she fed, often for free. Those were hard times back then.

That is the huge window I cleaned as a girl!

My mom, Celeste, who later became a celebrity in her own right (more on that later) ran the shop while Dad worked in the factory. After a few years, with my mom whipping up delicious foods such as fish fry every Friday and free manicotti on Saturday, they saved up enough money to open the Kedzie Beer Garden, a neighborhood tavern on Polk; I was born in the apartment up above. I think I am one of the few people who can say I was literally born in the restaurant business.

The original restaurant wasn't even Italian! We had corned beef and cabbage and fried chicken on the menu. Not your typical versions: Celeste's versions that brought in her southern Italian roots. You'll see some of her takes on American classics in this book. On St. Patrick's Day, we made pounds and pounds of corned beef and bushels of cabbage. We offered free meals to any friends who passed by.

It was a family operation. We (Emanuel [Willy], Pasquale, Anthony Jr., and I) were all put to work. As a 9-year-old, it was my job to clean the inside and outside of the tavern windows! Our customers became family and everyone had their usual table. After school, I'd jump behind the bar to eat my Blue Star chips and drink a shot glass full of beer. Yes, beer. In those days, this was allowed.

As the business grew into a popular restaurant, we changed the name to Celeste's to honor Mom. And my mom's ravioli were the talk of the town. We figured out how to mass-produce them

My brother Willy with Mama and Pat at a Quaker Oats event.

Celebrating my granddaughter Ali's Communion.

My granddaughter Jackie shares my love of baking.

Father David blessing the Clara's kitchen.

CULLINARY ARTS
THE PIZZA

CELESTE FROZEN PIZZA

MAMA CELESTE
BRINGS YOU THE OLD FAMILY

Being on Mama's float was a thrill.

This is me in the director's chair with my grandson Arturo.

Our Indiana mushroom haul, circa 1970! That's Aunt Marilyn, Mama, and Will.

"What dear and wonderful recipes and memories I want to share with you."

—Clara Lizio Melchiorre

Our original packaging, designed, in part, by me.

Rudy Jr. and I celebrating Clara's 30th anniversary.

Chapter 1

THE CUPBOARD

IN MY KITCHEN, THERE ARE a few things you have to keep on hand to be able to quickly make a delicious meal for your family. My son Rudy came up with the tagline *Salt, Pepper, Basil & Olive Oil*. I said, "And garlic and parsley, too!" Truthfully, you can make a lot of Italian food with just those ingredients. But there are a few more dry ingredients for the cupboard and others for the refrigerator that can open up a world of meals.

You'll start to see patterns in my recipes. Most of the savory dishes start with my garlic oil. Instead of just putting chopped garlic into hot oil, I batch garlic olive oil (page 20). For me, it adds depth to the dishes. Your cooking style and ingredients can be simple and yet as delicious as more elaborate preparations.

Cupboard

- **Pure olive oil:** I reserve extra-virgin for finishing my dishes
- **Vinegar:** I like a simple white wine vinegar, and a red wine vinegar by Colavita. Always go with a high acidity, like 6%
- **Aged balsamic vinegar:** for finishing
- **Basic balsamic vinegar**
- **Flat anchovies in olive oil**
- **Italian tuna in olive oil:** Cento or Genova brands
- **White wine:** Carlo Rossi chablis. It comes in a gallon!
- **Fine sea salt**
- **Coarse sea salt**
- **Kosher salt:** for brining
- **Coarse ground black pepper**
- **Canned beans:** kidney, chickpeas, white kidney beans (cannellini), red kidney beans
- **Dried 18-bean soup mix**
- **Dried lentils**
- **Canned whole peeled San Marzano tomatoes** (28-ounce can)
- **Tomato paste:** I always have Cento brand on hand
- **Seasoned breadcrumbs (homemade, page 30)**
- **Red pepper flakes:** You can get them from Costco in one big container
- **Dried oregano on the stem:** I don't really favor dried herbs; they're not in my repertoire. Oregano is different. I go for Mediterranean or Greek oregano, dried on the stem. After you strip the oregano leaves from the stems and measure your quantity, rub the oregano between your hands and smell the aroma. It's absolutely miraculous!
- **Pasta:** short and long
- **Canned black olives**
- **Sugar**
- **Unbleached Ceresota-brand flour:** Like my mom used
- **Cornmeal**
- **Risotto rice:** I prefer Vialone to Arborio

Fridge

- **Fresh flat-leaf Italian parsley**
- **Fresh basil**
- **Lemons**
- **Butter**
- **Garlic olive oil (page 20)**
- **Oil with peppers (page 22)**
- **Eggs**
- **Parmigiano-Reggiano, grated**
- **Sheep's milk cheese such as Pecorino Romano or Locatelli, chunk**
- **Parmigiano-Reggiano, chunk**

TIP: *I always keep a combo of salt and pepper on the stove. I do about 1 part black pepper to 5 parts fine sea salt. I keep another covered bowl with coarse sea salt. (I use this instead of kosher salt.) The third bowl is coarse red pepper.*

"Every good meal starts with good ingredients."

—Clara Lizio Melchiorre

GARLIC OLIVE OIL

This is used in various cooking preparations. My homemade garlic olive oil is much more versatile than the jarred chopped garlic you can buy. When you create more of an emulsion like this is, you can use it as a marinade or topping for steaks and chops. A rougher chop covered in oil replaces chopping garlic every time a recipe requires it.

INGREDIENTS

- 1 oz of garlic cloves, peeled and each clove cut into 3–4 pieces
- 4 cups of pure olive oil

PROCEDURE

Add garlic to your food processor. Start pulsing. Begin drizzling in olive oil a little at a time while the processor is running. Scrape down the sides to make sure no big pieces are left. Place in a glass bottle and just cover the top with olive oil. Either leave on your counter or pulse until more of an emulsion and store in the fridge.

How to Store Basil & Parsley, Two Ways

Basil adds flavor to recipes, while parsley adds freshness. I always have them on hand. To extend the life of the fresh herbs, I never wash until I'm ready to use basil and parsley. To store, I cut off a little from the bottom, place it in a glass of water, and put a baggie over it. I then store this in the fridge. The other way is I put it in a plastic baggie in the refrigerator drawer.

Measure Properly

When we sold Mama's company to Quaker Oats, we had a big problem. She never wrote down her recipes. Her hands were her measuring cups. Her fingers were her measuring spoons. She eyeballed everything! To get her recipes, the folks from Quaker Oats chased her around. She'd grab a fistful of flour, and they'd be right behind her with a scale to weigh it! This is how they got the measurements. As a cook, I weigh things, because four cloves of garlic in a recipe can have a lot of variation. I like accurate recipes.

NOTE: My recipes are by weight except where it's too cumbersome or unnecessary to weigh the ingredients.

WHICH KNIVES DO YOU *REALLY* NEED?

You might be surprised by the knives I use in my kitchen. I don't have a full set of fancy knives. I've collected different ones along the way. There are six knives that are essential.

1. **Santoku:** I bought Cutco knives from one of the waiters years ago. I love the santoku knife that came in the set.
2. **Chef's knife**
3. **Bread knife**
4. **Slicing knife**
5. **Boning knife**
6. **Paring knife**

HOT PEPPER OIL
(a.k.a. Michelle's Hot Oil Insanity)

If you like heat, this is a great oil to keep on hand. You fire up peppers in oil and store the oil in a jar. Mine was getting too hot, so I now blend sweet and hot peppers.

INGREDIENTS

- ½ cup olive oil
- 4 sweet banana peppers, sliced round with seeds
- 2 hot banana peppers, sliced round, with seeds
- 2 each poblano, serrano, and jalapeño peppers, cut in rounds
- 1 tsp. salt

PROCEDURE

Keep each type of pepper in a separate bowl. Heat oil in a frying pan. Add sweet peppers in one layer. Sprinkle with salt and sauté. Cook through. When you remove, place in a bowl. Repeat for all peppers. When done frying peppers, strain oil and let it cool down. Discard the peppers. You can store the oil in the fridge for several days, but it won't last a very long time.

TIP: *Serve with steak or on sandwiches.*

HOW TO BLANCH TOMATOES

At Clara's, all fresh tomatoes are peeled. It's small details like this that give dishes improved flavor.

PROCEDURE

Boil water in a pot that can fit one tomato at a time. Cross your tomatoes at the bottom. Get a bowl of ice water ready. Place the tomatoes on a spider (slotted spoon) and dunk in the boiling water for about 15–25 seconds, depending on size. Remove quickly and plunk into ice water so they stay firm. Core the tomato and peel.

TIP: *Never refrigerate tomatoes. Just buy them earlier than you need them, like 3 days before, and let them ripen on the countertop.*

Hatch the bottom.

You know it's ready when the skin starts to blister.

THE MOST BASIC SALAD DRESSING RECIPE

There's no need to get bottled dressing. At Celeste's we'd all make salad, but Mom's was uniquely the best one. We all added the same ingredients, but Mom's had the special touch of love. Mom's was always perfect.

INGREDIENTS

Lettuce: *I like a mix of lettuce, such as butter, arugula, and romaine*

Olive oil

Red vinegar

Salt

It's hard to do quantities here. You don't want to drown your salad; you want just enough dressing to coat the leaves. You never want a pool of dressing in the bottom of the bowl.

PROCEDURE

In a mixing bowl, add your salad mix. Sprinkle olive oil sparingly. Add red vinegar and toss with your hands. Sprinkle salt. Toss again.

Clara's Simple Caesar Dressing

INGREDIENTS

1½ oz garlic cloves, peeled
2 oz anchovies
3 Tbsp sweet spiced mustard
12 oz Parmigiano-Reggiano
30 oz olive oil
6 oz fresh lemon juice
Pinch of salt and black pepper

PROCEDURE

In a large food processor, place the garlic and pulse. Add anchovies, mustard, Parmigiano, lemon juice, and salt and pepper. Allow to blend together. Drizzle in olive oil and allow mixture to emulsify.

VINEGAR PEPPERS

INGREDIENTS

- ½ gallon white vinegar
- ½ gallon water
- ½ cup salt
- Assortment of hot peppers: banana peppers, finger-long hot peppers, serranos, jalapeños, and cubanos, depending on how hot you like *(Make sure there are no blemishes or holes in the peppers)*
- Dry oregano on the stem
- 5–6 whole garlic cloves, peeled and stem removed, per quart jar
- 4 1-quart canning jars

PROCEDURE

In a heavy-bottomed pot, bring the vinegar and water to a boil. Add salt and allow to boil for 5–7 minutes. Then turn off the heat and allow to cool. Wash the hot peppers, dry them, and snip off the tip of each stem. Firmly pack peppers in each jar, alternating stem up and stem down to fit in more peppers. Add 5–6 oregano stems with branches attached as you add peppers, plus 5–6 garlic cloves. Pour the cooled liquid (vinegar and water) over top of the peppers, oregano, and garlic. Fill jars to ½ inch from the top. Seal with lid and ring. Invert jars and place on a tray overnight. The next day, turn them over, label, and store for future use. Can be refrigerated and used 2 weeks later. Will fill approximately four 1-quart jars.

HOMEMADE BREADCRUMBS

INGREDIENTS

12–16 oz stale Italian bread, cut into 1-inch pieces

1 Tbsp salt

½ Tbsp black pepper

4 oz grated Parmigiano-Reggiano

4 oz grated Romano cheese

4 oz coarsely chopped parsley

1 Tbsp chopped garlic

PROCEDURE

Take your leftover crusty Italian bread. Using the grater attachment on your food processor, grate the bread. Put the crumbs in a bowl. Add the remaining ingredients. Blend together. Store in a zip-top bag in the fridge. They stay well in the fridge, even more than a month! Yields about 3 cups of breadcrumbs.

TIP: *Store your leftover bread in the pantry to use later for breadcrumbs.*

HOW TO FRY IN PURE OLIVE OIL
(without burning)

Start oil on medium heat; don't turn the flame all the way up. Bring the temperature up to around 350°F, slowly. Always stay with your oil. This way, your olive oil won't burn.

the weekend. I saw he had a pastry bag and he was squeezing the cookies out just like stuffing for the ravioli. I asked, "Can you get me one of those?"

I thought about how much time I could save if I put the ravioli filling in a pastry bag instead of scooping 120 tablespoons of filling. That night at the restaurant, I revolutionized ravioli-making! My mom, of course, said, "You're going to ruin the ravioli," when she saw the bag. I persevered and used it. To this day we still use the pastry bag—even for lasagna.

> ## "You're going to ruin the ravioli!"
> —Celeste Lizio, Clara's mom

We started making mass quantities of ravioli and selling to local restaurants. It was 12 ravioli for 98 cents for home cooks at local stores. Five dozen boxes went to restaurants. The first night we were at the plant working, we didn't have a logo. I told my brothers we needed a silhouette of Mama. So I took a light bulb and did a silhouette of her against the wall. Remember that trick? We printed it and stapled it to the packaging.

I remember after a demonstration, the deli manager at a local store asked, "Do you think you're going to go anywhere with this business?" I don't think any of us knew the answer at that point. From that humble beginning of making our own pasta, we created a production line and began selling

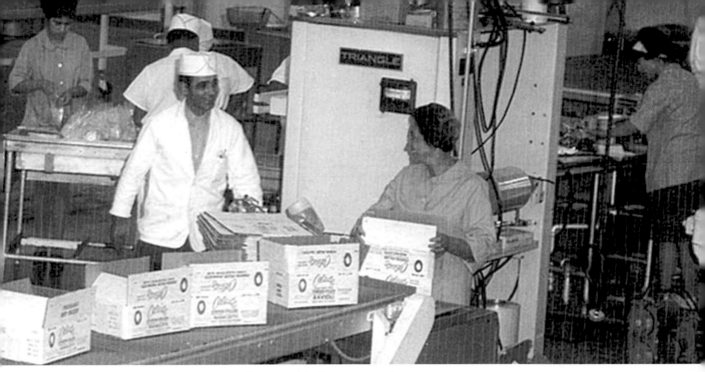

An early assembly line at our plant.

all over Chicago. The family restaurant was successful, but we wanted to get bigger or do something else, but didn't know what. We decided to shut the restaurant and focus on pasta manufacturing.

Twenty years later, I was back in the pasta business with Clara's. We were a pasta restaurant but didn't have a proper pasta machine—just the one Mom and Dad brought from Italy. We could make linguine and fettuccine only. When we opened, that's what we served. We finally bought our first professional pasta machine from Cora Imports. (We still buy from them.) We could make more than a pound of pasta at a time!

We didn't have enough power or room to operate it, though. Thank goodness for our neighbors in the strip mall. Frannie and Ray owned a hairdressing shop. They had an empty room in the back. We set up our pasta machine there.

Here are some of my favorite pasta* recipes, many adapted from the restaurant, for you to enjoy at home with family.

All recipes for 1 lb of dry pasta serve a family of four, unless otherwise indicated.

FETTUCCINE ALFREDO

This one is a favorite of so many customers! It's not the most heart-healthy, but it's the most outstanding Alfredo you will ever taste.

INGREDIENTS
   10 oz butter, softened
   6 oz grated Parmigiano-Reggiano
   16 oz heavy cream

PROCEDURE
In a tall, 8-quart heavy-bottomed pot, fill with water to even with handles. Begin heating water over medium-low heat. Put softened butter in food processor fastened with a metal blade and pulse to blend. Add grated Parmigiano-Reggiano to food processor and pulse to blend into softened butter. With a rubber spatula, scrape down sides of food processor. Allow food processor to run until mixture is light and fluffy, then set aside when done. Place an 8-quart sauce pot over medium-high heat. Add heavy cream and the Parmigiano-Reggiano butter mixture to pot, stir to blend sauce together, then continue stirring frequently to prevent sauce from sticking to the bottom. As sauce thickens, lower to medium heat. Raise pasta water to high heat and bring to a boil. As pasta water starts to boil, add 2 tablespoons of sea salt, then add pasta. Remove pasta from water 2 minutes before recommended cooking time, strain pasta and allow to drain well. Add pasta to Alfredo sauce and stir thoroughly. Allow pasta to cook the remaining 2 minutes in the sauce. Serve and enjoy!

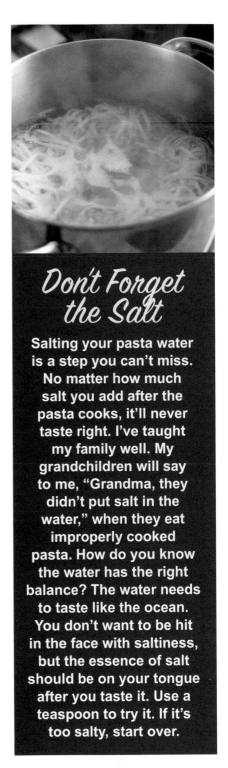

Don't Forget the Salt

Salting your pasta water is a step you can't miss. No matter how much salt you add after the pasta cooks, it'll never taste right. I've taught my family well. My grandchildren will say to me, "Grandma, they didn't put salt in the water," when they eat improperly cooked pasta. How do you know the water has the right balance? The water needs to taste like the ocean. You don't want to be hit in the face with saltiness, but the essence of salt should be on your tongue after you taste it. Use a teaspoon to try it. If it's too salty, start over.

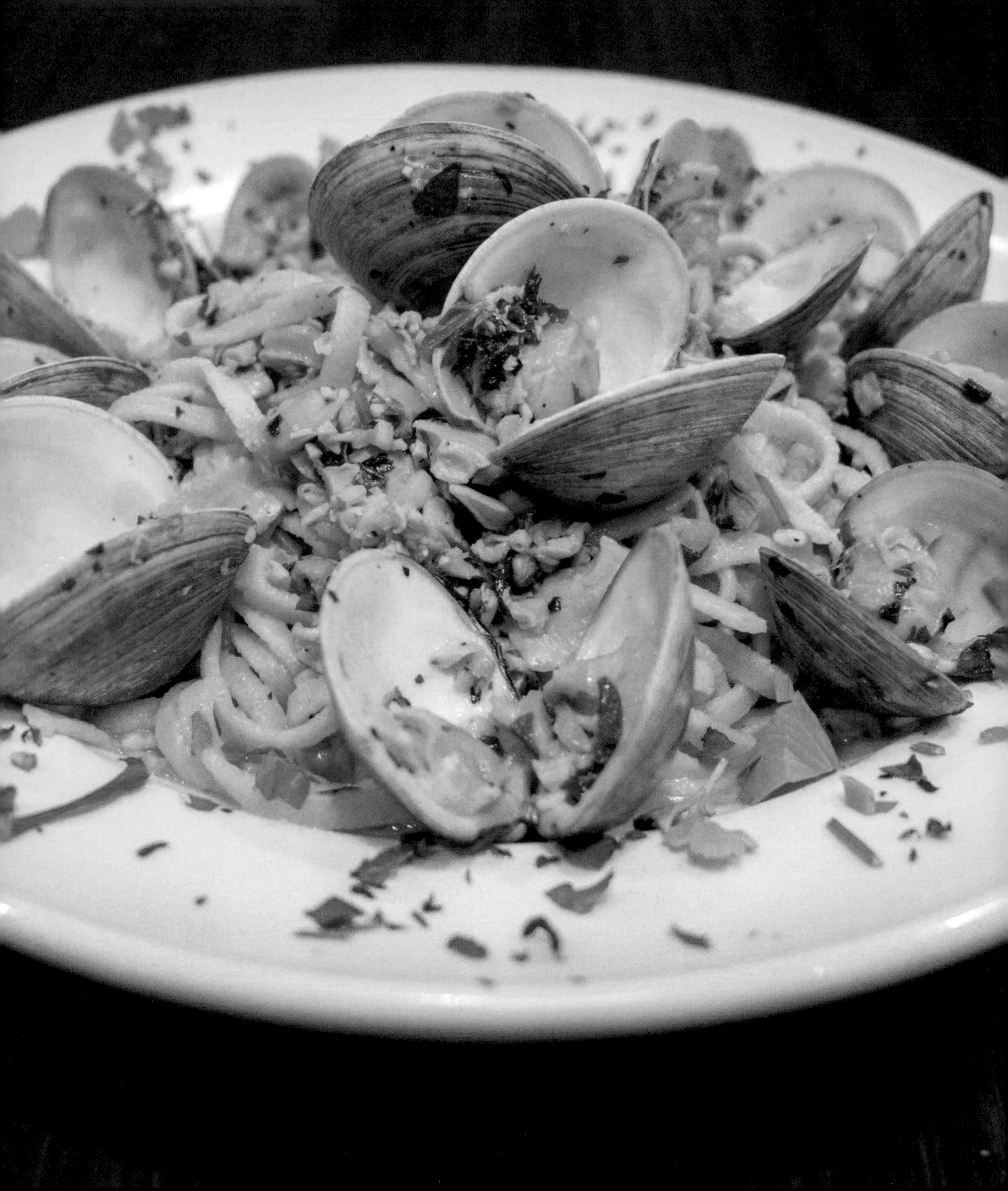

CLAM SAUCE TWO WAYS

At Clara's, my husband would pick the busiest times to eat his dinners!

INGREDIENTS (FOR BOTH SAUCES)

½ lb linguine *(recommended; any pasta works)*

1½ tsp olive oil

2 Tbsp garlic purée (page 20)

2 Tbsp fresh parsley

13 oz clams in juice (2 6.5 oz cans) *(drain juices but keep in separate bowl)*

¼ tsp basil

¼ tsp oregano

Pinch of crushed red pepper

Salt and pepper to taste

½ cup white wine

For red sauce:

4 Tbsp San Marzano whole peeled tomatoes, crushed by hand **or in a blender** *(for a smoother sauce, process tomatoes longer)*

PROCEDURE

In a medium saucepan on medium heat, add oil. Add garlic purée, let dance. Add parsley to coat garlic. Add drained clams. Add seasonings; sauté. (If making red sauce, this is where you add the crushed tomatoes.) Add wine, let simmer. Most of the wine should be dissolved, about 3 minutes. Add the juices from the clams. Simmer about 2 minutes. Add drained pasta to clam sauce and serve. Serves 2.

TIP: *This dish can be made with fresh clams! Do this as your first step: Clean sand from clams by soaking in saltwater and scrubbing the shells, then sauté clams in oil until they pop, and remove. Add back when you finish the last step of the recipe.*

Clara's Fresh VEGGIE MARINARA SAUCE

Once you lovingly prep your veggies, this sauce cooks quickly. It's truly worth your time and effort. After all, the main ingredient is your love! Another great thing about this recipe is that you can be as creative as you like—mix and add your favorite veggies and create your own unique sauce.

INGREDIENTS

- ¾ cup pure olive oil
- 3 large fresh garlic cloves
- 2 slender medium zucchini
- 2 slender medium yellow squash
- 3 large ribs celery
- 2 carrots
- 1 slender leek
- 1 28-oz can San Marzano peeled whole tomatoes
- 1 lb white mushrooms
- 1 cup dry white wine
- Salt and black pepper to taste
- Dry red pepper flakes (optional)
- ½ bunch fresh parsley (leaves only)
- 1 packet fresh basil (leaves only)

PROCEDURE

You'll need a large, heavy-bottomed sauté pan or pot to accommodate all of the ingredients. Prepare all veggies: Finely chop garlic. Quarter-cut zucchini and cut yellow squash lengthwise, then in quarter-inch slices. Dice-cut celery; julienne-cut or dice carrots. Wash leek well and thinly slice. Coarsely chop tomatoes. Wipe mushrooms and cut in quarter-inch slices. Coarsely chop parsley and basil. Heat olive oil in pan over medium heat. Add garlic and leek; stir with wooden spoon. Add carrot and celery. Sprinkle a touch of salt and pepper. Stir in zucchini, squash, and mushrooms; add another sprinkle of salt and pepper. Next, add tomatoes and white wine and stir. Allow to come to a soft boil, then simmer until veggies are tender. Do a taste check to see if it needs more salt or pepper. If you like it spicy, add dry red pepper flakes to taste. Turn off heat and stir in fresh parsley and basil.

Marinara with Tuna

INGREDIENTS

2 Tbsp olive oil

1 medium onion, chopped

2 Tbsp garlic purée

2 5-oz cans high-quality Italian tuna (tonno) packed in olive oil *(Genova or Cento brands are great)*

1 28-oz can San Marzano tomatoes

Splash of dry white wine

¼ tsp sea salt

¼ tsp pepper

¼ tsp crushed red pepper

2 Tbsp fresh parsley, chopped

1 Tbsp fresh basil, chopped *(1 tsp if you only have dried)*

PROCEDURE

In a large pot on medium heat, add oil. Sauté onion and garlic. Add tuna, tomatoes, and wine. Add seasonings, fresh parsley and basil. Stir well. Cover and turn down heat to low. Cook covered for at least 40 minutes, stirring occasionally. Serve over your favorite pasta.

The Gravy Recipe!

INGREDIENTS
- 3 lbs bone-in country ribs
- 1 pinch salt
- 1 pinch pepper
- ¼ cup olive oil
- 1 medium/large onion
- 3–4 large garlic cloves
- 1 handful fresh chopped parsley
- 2 28-oz whole tomatoes *(break apart with your hands in a bowl or purée—whatever texture you prefer)*
- 2 cups white wine

PROCEDURE
Rinse ribs in cold water and pat dry. Add salt and pepper to a heavy-bottomed pot. Heat olive oil, brown all sides of ribs and set aside. Chop onion and garlic cloves into pieces. Add chopped

onion and garlic to oil, sauté until translucent. Add a handful of chopped fresh parsley. Blend in tomatoes and add white wine. Return pork to gravy and simmer for 2 hours.

THE SAUCE GLOSSARY

SAUCE OR SALSA: In Italian, *salsa* means *sauce*, usually tomato sauce. Tomatoes aren't even native to Italy. They were brought to Italy by the conquistadors in the mid-16th century.

MARINARA: This is a chunky, Neapolitan sauce traditionally made with onion, tomato, and oregano. The story says it was made by wives waiting for their husbands (the *marinari*) to get home from fishing. My "marinara" refers to a quickly cooked tomato sauce.

RAGÙ: This means it's a meat sauce. Different parts of Italy make their own ragùs. In Tuscany, you see wild boar ragù. And in Bologna, you get possibly the most famous ragù, made with a mix of ground meat and delicately simmered for hours. In Naples, it's made with larger cuts of meat, lots of onion and basil. My meat sauce (at left) is my own take on ragù.

WHAT ABOUT GRAVY? Gravy is commonly used by Italian-Americans to describe various tomato-based sauces, but it's usually synonymous for the rich Neapolitan, meat-based sauce. Go to page 81 for my famous Gravy Sandwich recipe.

BUCATINI all'AMATRICIANA

I don't do anything special to this classic recipe. It is perfect just the way it is.

INGREDIENTS

- ¼ cup olive oil
- 12 oz thinly sliced guanciale, pancetta, or bacon
- 1 red onion, cut lengthwise in half and into ¼-inch-thick half-moon slices
- 3 garlic cloves, sliced
- 1½ tsp hot red pepper flakes
- 2 cups simple tomato sauce (page 48)
- 1 lb bucatini
- Freshly grated Pecorino Romano cheese

PROCEDURE

In a 10- or 12-inch sauté pan, combine olive oil, guanciale, onion, garlic, and red pepper flakes. Set to low heat. Cook until onion is softened and guanciale has rendered much of its fat, about 12 minutes. Drain off all but ¼ cup of fat. *(Tip: Set aside extra fat to cook eggs for tomorrow's breakfast.)* Add tomato sauce and bring to a boil. Then lower to a simmer. Allow to bubble for 6–7 minutes. Put your pasta bowls into a 140°F oven to warm. While sauce simmers, cook bucatini for about a minute less than package directions (make sure it is still very firm), then drain the pasta. Toss drained pasta into sauce and cook for about a minute. Divide pasta in heated bowl. Top with freshly grated Pecorino Romano. Serve immediately.

Gnocchi!

Gnocchi always reminds me of my husband, Rudy. He and I lived parallel lives for years without ever meeting. We grew up in close proximity, knew a lot of the same people, even crossed over at Marquette for a year. We finally met when I went to his sister Mary's dress shop. When I got there, my future sister-in-law called her brother and said, "'The gnocchi is here.'" He raced over. He became the love of my life. I along with pasta were his favorites.

QUICK GNOCCHI (a.k.a. Nudi)

INGREDIENTS

1 lb ricotta
1 cup Parmigiano-Reggiano

Salt and pepper
1½ cups flour

PROCEDURE

In a bowl, add ricotta, Parmigiano-Reggiano, salt, pepper, and flour. Mix thoroughly. Roll gnocchi into walnut-size pieces. Place on tray. In small batches, boil the gnocchi in water for 3–4 minutes. Place gnocchi in tomato sauce or melted butter. Sprinkle with additional Parmigiano-Reggiano. Bake until bubbly, 10–12 minutes.

TIP: *Serve tossed in simple tomato sauce (page 48).*

POTATO GNOCCHI

INGREDIENTS

6 eggs, beaten

20 Idaho potatoes, boiled and riced

3 tsp salt

Flour to thicken and work the dough

PROCEDURE

In a large bowl, fold the eggs into the potatoes. Add the salt. Flour a clean surface. Mix with your hands until the dough starts to clump together. Once you can form a ball, transfer it to the floured surface. Knead gently until the flour is fully incorporated and the dough is soft, smooth, and a little sticky, 30 seconds to 1 minute. Don't overmix or the gnocchi will be tough. Cut off a piece of the dough and roll out into a long strip. Using a sharp knife or bench knife, cut ¼-inch pieces. Once cut, place on a floured cookie sheet. Sprinkle with flour. The gnocchi will cook quickly when added to your boiling salted water. When they rise to the top, they are ready!

PASTA FAGIOLI

This soul-warming pasta dish is a classic in Italian cooking. Every Italian cook has their own special touch. For me, it's using flat Great Northern beans, which are larger than navy beans and smaller than cannellini beans but have a more delicate flavor.

INGREDIENTS

2 lbs Great Northern beans

1/3 cup olive oil

Mince the following:

1 medium onion

6 cloves garlic

3 carrots

4 ribs celery

1 red pepper, seeded

Salt and pepper

1 can tomato paste

Parsley to taste

Basil to taste

1 lb ditalini pasta

1 cup Parmigiano-Reggiano, grated

PROCEDURE

Make the beans: Place beans in a large pot filled with cold water to cover, about 3 inches above beans. Bring to a boil, then reduce to low boil. Cook until tender. Remove beans and reserve cooking water. In a large pan, heat olive oil. Add onion and garlic and sauté until garlic dances. Add carrots, celery, red pepper, 1 teaspoon salt and ½ teaspoon black pepper. Place tomato paste in a bowl and make a slurry by adding bean water. Pour slurry into the vegetables; add more water if needed to create a thick soup. Reduce heat to a simmer until vegetables are soft. Add beans and continue cooking about 30–45 minutes.

Make the pasta: In a pot of salted water, cook the ditalini. When al dente—or still slightly firm—strain. Cool pasta, then add to the bean soup mixture. Add parsley, basil, liberal amounts of Parmigiano-Reggiano and salt and black pepper to taste. This dish is soul-warming.

My son Mark's variation uses red onion. And he sautées about ⅓ cup of cubed bacon, pancetta or guanciale till "chewy" in a separate pan. He then adds to the bean mixture before reducing the heat. I always encourage him (and you) to make the dish your own.

MAKE THE PERFECT PASTA DOUGH

I remember as a young child, my mom always made pasta by hand. We made ravioli twice a week. She would begin by doing a well of flour, breaking her eggs and incorporating. This is still how pasta is made in Italy. We would make 5 pounds of dough at a time! We'll do a bit less for this at-home recipe. But it's still a labor of love, though just 3 ingredients: flour, eggs, your hands.

INGREDIENTS
1 lb flour
5 large eggs, at room temperature

PROCEDURE
Make the dough: Make a well or volcano out of the flour. Crack in the eggs one by one. Using a fork, beat the eggs inside the well. Begin incorporating flour from the sides. *(Tip: If your volcano leaks, don't worry. Just patch it up with some flour.)* Once enough of the egg is incorporated

(it's not runny), gather the rest of the flour into the dough and pat it. Use a bench scraper to pick up all the pieces. *(Tip: Don't worry about sticky hands. The dough will get incorporated.)* With your hands, bring it toward you, then push away with the heels of your hands. Quarter-turn toward you, heels away. Do this a couple of times. Dough should be easily kneaded. If it's too wet, add a little more flour. In a few minutes, it should look smooth. Roll the dough into a ball, flatten a tad, and wrap in lightly floured plastic wrap. Let it rest for 30 minutes.

Roll the pasta: After it rests, use a bench cutter to cut the dough into quarters. Keep unused portion wrapped. Flatten out your quarter on a lightly floured surface. Start to roll out your dough with a roller. Forward and back. Turn dough quarter turns after a couple of rolls in each direction. Flour as needed—very little, just to prevent it from sticking to the pin. Constantly do quarter turns until the dough is very thin, about 1/16th of an inch. I'll be honest here, a hand-crank machine that you can buy inexpensively online can make this rolling phase much easier.

Cut the pasta: Flour your thin sheet of dough. Lightly flour and roll it on top of itself a few times. Using a sharp knife, cut to the desired thickness of the pasta. Pappardelle are your widest at about ¾ inch, fettuccine and linguine are thinner. Place on a lightly floured, clean tea towel or tablecloth and cover pasta while it dries. If you aren't going to serve that day, place in a zip-top bag and freeze.

How to Make
RICOTTA FILLING

This is a simple way to dress your ricotta for baked pasta or a ravioli/ lasagna filling.

INGREDIENTS

6 lbs ricotta

1¾ Tbsp sea salt

1 Tbsp black pepper

1¾ cups Pecorino Romano cheese

1 handful freshly chopped parsley and basil

8 beaten eggs

2 cups shredded mozzarella

PROCEDURE

Combine all ingredients in a large bowl. Cover with plastic wrap and refrigerate until ready to use.

RAVIOLI

1 pound of filling (page 55) will make about 2 dozen ravioli.

PROCEDURE

Lay two long pasta sheets (see page 52 for fresh pasta recipe) on a large, floured surface. Using a pastry bag (or spoon), place about 1½ tablespoons of filling for each raviolo in two rows on the sheet. Leave about ¼ inch on all sides. Using a brush dipped in water, dab water around the outer edges and the inner edges.

Take your second sheet and place it on top. Push down around your ravioli and, using a pastry cutter or even a sharp knife, cut your ravioli. Place on a floured tea towel and cover with another towel. Repeat with additional sheets.

COOKING FRESH PASTA

When you cook any fresh pasta, it is pretty quick. Bring salted water to a boil and drop the pasta in. When it comes back to a boil, lower the heat. Stir gently with a spider or slotted spoon. The pasta should be ready in 3–5 minutes or when it rises to the top.

THE "ORIGINAL" PESTO SAUCE

Pesto is a recipe from Genoa, Italy—pretty far from Naples. I learned how to make a true pesto Genovese from Vince Casuello, who came from there. When my uncles went to New York to buy pasta machines, they sent Vince to watch over things. He never left! Maybe it just seemed that way because he was always around. He eventually opened his own pasta business. And in the early days of Clara's, when we needed a liquor license, he showed up with $5,000 in a brown bag for us to pay for it.

INGREDIENTS

- 5 large garlic cloves
- 1 lb basil (destemmed and cleaned)
- 1 cup Parmigiano-Reggiano
- ½ cup Pecorino Romano cheese
- ½ cup lightly toasted pignoli (pine nuts)
- Salt to taste
- 2 cups olive oil

PROCEDURE

Mince garlic in processor. Add basil and blend. Add cheese ½ cup at a time. Slowly add olive oil in a stream. Add pine nuts and salt to taste. If it's too dry, add more oil.

TIP: *Make this nut-free by simply omitting the pignoli.*

RISOTTO WITH MUSHROOMS

INGREDIENTS

- **8 cups mushrooms, quartered** *(I like a mixture of button, cremini, shiitake, and maitake. Use your favorites.)*
- **1 medium onion, chopped**
- **1 Tbsp garlic olive oil (page 20)**
- **6 Tbsp olive oil to coat the bottom of the pan**
- **1 cup Arborio rice (Italian rice)**
- **1 cup white wine**
- **4 cups chicken broth**
- **⅓ cup grated Parmigiano-Reggiano**
- **Black pepper to taste**

PROCEDURE

Clean and dry mushrooms with a paper towel. Do not rinse mushrooms, as they will absorb water. Place in a bowl with garlic olive oil and toss. In a large saucepan on medium-high heat, add enough oil to cover the bottom of the pan. In batches, cook the mushrooms until they begin to crisp. Once done, remove mushrooms and set aside. Add oil as needed per batch. The mushrooms will absorb the oil. When all the mushrooms are cooked and set aside, keep the remaining oil in the pan. Scrape the mushroom residue on the bottom to avoid burning. Add more oil if needed. Add onions and sauté until translucent. Add Arborio rice. Stir into onions. Cook 2 minutes, stirring continuously. Add wine and continue stirring continuously to avoid rice sticking to the bottom of the pan. The rice will absorb the liquid. Once wine is absorbed, we'll begin adding chicken broth. This is a slow process that will take continuous stirring. Add ½ cup of chicken stock at a time. Let absorb, and repeat until rice is done. Add Parmigiano-Reggiano and pepper. Blend into rice. Add cooked mushrooms. Blend into rice. Transfer to a serving dish. Garnish with more Parmigiano-Reggiano.

Chapter 3
"OFF" THE MENU

Rudy and I at the Clara's bar—
*two-drink **maximum** was his rule.*

I'LL NEVER FORGET THE QUESTION Eileen Nysson, the town clerk, asked when I went to apply for my first restaurant permit: "Do you really think you should open a restaurant here?" Two restaurants had previously failed in that space. I know Eileen was just looking out for me back in 1987. Every year after that, until she retired, I'd joke with her, "Think I should open here?"

I finally decided to open my own place. I called it Clara's Pasta

> ## "Do you really think you should open a restaurant here?"
>
> —*Eileen Nysson, Town Clerk*

di Casa (Clara's Housemade Pasta). In my mind, I was opening a special treasure. Our customers were family coming to our "home" for dinner. Pasta prepared to order was our thing. Those were wonderful years.

Why did I finally venture out on my own? You know life has its ups and downs. I had left the family business; my husband was doing well as a real estate developer. Then we hit a down. I didn't let that hold us back. My mom, Celeste, gave me a loan to get started. We opened in the space of a shuttered Japanese restaurant called Osaka Joe's. It was 30 minutes west of Chicago on Route 53, not a picturesque site.

The decor was definitely not Italian! We had Japanese lanterns, Asian bowls, and cases of Sapporo beer. We thought Clara's was

My Version of BRUSCHETTA

INGREDIENTS
- 4 large tomatoes, blanched (page 24)
- 2 Tbsp pesto (page 58)
- ½ cup Fontinella cheese, coarsely chopped
- Salt and pepper
- 2 Tbsp olive oil
- 1 loaf of garlic bread (see below)

PROCEDURE

Chop blanched tomatoes. Place in a strainer to get the juices out. (This is the base of your bruschetta.) Blend tomatoes, pesto, Fontinella, salt, and pepper. Add a generous dollop of the tomato mixture to a warm slice of garlic bread. Drizzle with olive oil.

Simplest Garlic Bread Ever

Toast French bread cut lengthwise, and gently rub a clove of garlic on it while bread is warm.

My Mom's Version of
LASAGNA

*Use a 12" wide × 16" long × 3.5" deep pan. If you want
to make it vegetarian, skip the meat mixture.*

INGREDIENTS

- **LASAGNA NOODLES: Make lasagna sheets using the dough recipe on page 52. You can cut the sheets into squares, which will be easier to fit in the bottom of your pan.** *(Tip: If you're short on time, you can use the store-bought no-boil lasagna, or the long, curly ones you boil.)*

- **GRAVY: Use your basic tomato sauce (page 48) or meat sauce (page 42).**

- **RICOTTA FILLING**

2 lbs ricotta	**½ bunch of Italian flat parsley leaves, coarsely chopped**
½ cup Romano cheese	
½ lb grated mozzarella	**1 oz basil**
½ Tbsp salt	**4 eggs**
½ tsp pepper	

  Combine all ingredients in a large bowl.

- **MEAT MIXTURE**

1½ lbs of ground beef *(or any 1½ lbs of meat. You can use a beef/pork/veal combo or turkey. It's really up to your taste.)*	**2 large garlic cloves, chopped**
	¼ cup Romano cheese
	Fresh parsley, chopped
½ Tbsp sea salt	**Fresh basil, chopped**
¼ Tbsp coarse black pepper	**2 eggs**

  Brown the meat. Drain the fat. When cooled down, mix in the other ingredients. At the restaurant, we liked to use a potato masher to give a smoother texture to the mixture.

- **2 CUPS OF SHREDDED FRESH MOZZARELLA**

Assemble the lasagna: Spray bottom of baking tray. Layer sauce on the bottom of pan. Next, add your first layer of pasta. Then layer your ricotta filling, then a layer of ground beef. Sprinkle shredded fresh mozzarella. Add several dollops of sauce. Repeat for three layers of pasta. On your final layer, top with sauce and mozzarella.

Bake the lasagna: Preheat oven to 400°F. Place a baking tray, covered with foil, on bottom rack to catch drippings. Cover lasagna tightly with foil and place in oven over tray. Bake covered lasagna for 30 minutes. Rotate pan (back to front). Bake an additional 30 minutes until internal temperature is 140°F. Remove lasagna from the oven. Generously sprinkle additional fresh shredded mozzarella and distribute it well. Return to oven uncovered and bake until mozzarella is melted, golden brown, and bubbly.

Clara's in the '80s, Clara's today

LASAGNA FLORENTINE

What makes this very special is an abundance of spinach, béchamel, and spinach-flavored pasta. I came up with the recipe when a customer asked for spinach lasagna. For this variation, you replace the meat with sautéed spinach, lasagna noodles with spinach lasagna noodles (although regular noodles work the same), and the sauce with béchamel (except for the bottom layer).

INGREDIENTS

1 cup simple tomato sauce (page 48)

1 lb lasagna noodles, spinach-flavored

2 lbs ricotta filling (page 55)

2 lbs of spinach sautéed in garlic oil

Béchamel (see recipe, below)

1 lb mozzarella, shredded

For the béchamel:

½ lb flour

½ lb butter

½ gallon milk

¼ cup wine

Parmigiano-Reggiano to taste

Make the béchamel: Make a roux with butter and flour in a large saucepan over medium-low heat, stirring constantly with a wooden spoon. Slowly stir in the milk. Add the wine. Bring to a simmer, stirring constantly, and it will start to thicken. Whisk in Parmigiano-Reggiano. Season with salt and pepper.

Assemble the lasagna: Spray bottom of baking tray. Layer sauce on the bottom of pan. Next, add your first layer of pasta. Then layer your ricotta filling, then a layer of sautéed spinach. Sprinkle shredded fresh mozzarella. Add several dollops of béchamel. Repeat for three layers of pasta. On your final layer, top with béchamel and mozzarella.

CLARA'S SEAFOOD SPECIAL
(a.k.a. Zuppa di Pesce)

My husband, Rudy Sr., ran the front of the house—but that didn't stop him from eating his dinner and watching whatever game happened to be on. For two years straight, he ate Zuppa di Pesce every night. He'd give the waitresses a hard time but always tipped them $20.

INGREDIENTS

2 Tbsp olive oil

1½ lb Manila clams

1 lb fresh mussels, cleaned and debearded

¼ lb calamari rings

8 jumbo brown shrimp, cleaned, deveined

8 U15-grade sea scallops

2 Tbsp garlic emulsion (page 20)
(Option: Use tomato sauce in place of garlic emulsion.)

1 Tbsp fresh parsley, chopped

1 14.5-oz can crushed tomatoes

1 cup dry white wine

½ tsp hot pepper oil (page 22)

Salt and pepper to taste

1 lb linguine, cooked according to package directions

PROCEDURE

You will add fish one at a time, based on cooking time, and remove before adding the next. Heat 2 tablespoons of olive oil in a heavy-bottomed pot. When it starts to sizzle, add the clams and cover the pot with a lid to steam. As clams start to open, remove and add mussels. As they open, remove and add calamari. Repeat for shrimp and scallops. At the end, add the garlic emulsion (or add tomato sauce, if using instead). When it starts to dance, add parsley. Add crushed tomatoes. Let cook for 2 minutes and add back the fish. Add white wine and hot pepper oil. Add salt and pepper to taste. Cook until fish has flavored the sauce, or about 5 minutes. Toss linguine in seafood sauce, directly in pan. Serve immediately.

PASTA PRIMAVERA

This light pasta is a favorite of customers at Clara's. The traditional pasta is farfalle, but here a Casarecce, which cooks more evenly than farfalle, is used. Fresh veggies—broccoli, zucchini, carrots, mushrooms, and peapods are sautéed in herb garlic oil. Incredible!!!

INGREDIENTS

1 lb **Casarecce** *(or short pasta of your choice)*

3 Tbsp **garlic olive oil** *(page 20)*

1 lb **broccoli florets** *(about 1 broccoli crown)*

1 cup **carrots, julienned**

8 oz **button mushrooms, sliced**

1 medium **zucchini, julienned**

4 oz **peapods**

½ cup **white wine or reserved pasta water**

Salt and pepper to taste

FOR ALFREDO BUTTER

2 Tbsp **butter, softened**

2 Tbsp **grated Parmigiano-Reggiano, plus extra for serving**

Handful of fresh basil, thinly sliced

PROCEDURE

While your pasta water boils, heat the garlic olive oil in a large sauté pan. Add vegetables, one at a time, in the order listed above (hold the peapods), allowing a minute or two between vegetables. You can add a little bit of wine to each vegetable to help with cooking. Season with salt and pepper after each vegetable. Sauté over medium heat until soft, about 7 minutes. Add the peapods and give them a good stir. Turn off the stove and do not cover the veggies. Blend softened butter with 2 tablespoons of Parmigiano-Reggiano to make the Alfredo butter. When you are getting ready to drain the pasta, turn heat back to low on the vegetables. Add drained pasta to the sauté pan. Raise heat to high. Add Alfredo butter and remaining wine (or reserved pasta water) a tablespoon at a time to help coat the pasta. Place on a warmed platter and top with grated cheese and fresh basil. Serves 4, with lunch for one the next day.

MAKE IT A MEAL: You can add about a pound of chicken breast cut into small pieces or a pound of medium-size shrimp (tails off) to this pasta to make a delightful one-dish dinner. Start by sautéing your protein in garlic olive oil. Season with salt and pepper. About a third of the way through cooking, start the above recipe.

SHRIMP ERSILIA

My son Rudy Jr. came up with this dish and named it after his only daughter, my granddaughter Ersilia—Sisi, as we call her. It brings together so much of what I like to think I taught him about cooking—mise en place, fresh, good ingredients, lots of flavor. What gives this dish such great taste is that you season each ingredient as you move along in the recipe. So you're building flavor upon flavor.

INGREDIENTS

5 oz olive oil

1 oz garlic purée

4 Tbsp freshly chopped parsley

16 oz raw shrimp, cleaned

Salt and pepper *(keep handy throughout the cooking process)*

2 large whole portobello mushrooms, thinly sliced

4 oz sun-dried tomatoes *(dried or in oil; either is OK)*, **cut into slices**

1 cup (2 oz) cheese blend (Asiago, Romano, Fontinella, Parmigiano)

16 oz heavy cream

10 oz fresh spinach (two 5-oz bags)

1 lb cooked pasta *(angel hair or spaghettini recommended, but any pasta will work)*

PROCEDURE

This is a step-by-step process—do not add all ingredients at once. In a large frying pan on medium heat, add oil; let it get hot. Add garlic and let it start to dance. Add parsley. Next, add shrimp; salt and pepper to season and cook until about halfway done. Add portobello mushrooms; salt and pepper to season, cook until the mushrooms are tender. Add the sun-dried tomatoes. Then add the four-cheese blend; stir until coated. Add the heavy cream; simmer. The cream will become a darkened color; turn off heat. Add spinach; salt and pepper to season; wilt lightly. In pan, push all ingredients to one side so that you have the cream on the other. Add pasta to cream side. Toss. To plate, place pasta, then place remaining ingredients on top. If desired, add extra cheese on top for presentation.

TRADITIONAL CANNOLI

INGREDIENTS
- 3 lbs ricotta
- 2 cups sifted powdered sugar
- ¾ cup mini chocolate chips
- 12 premade cannoli shells

PROCEDURE

Combine ricotta and sugar until well blended. Add chocolate chips. Store covered in the fridge until ready to use. Stuff cannoli shells using a pastry bag—fill one side first, then turn cannoli and fill the other—just before serving, to avoid soggy shells.

Clara's Cannoli Dip!

Instead of stuffing the shells, you can break them into chips and serve with a bowl of sweet ricotta cream (cannoli cream).

Traditional Sicilian cannoli have the ends dipped in chopped pistachio nuts—you can also dip in additional mini chocolate chips.

TIRAMISU

We were doing a wedding at the restaurant. The chocolate cake was from Portillo's, but I had to make the tiramisu. I didn't like what was out there because of the heavy liquors. My option was to use a trio of coffee-flavored liqueurs.

INGREDIENTS

4 tsp Medaglia d'Oro instant espresso

1½ cups water

3 oz powdered sugar

5 egg yolks

4 oz granulated sugar

¼ tsp cream of tartar

5 egg whites

½ pint heavy cream

½ oz vanilla bean paste or pure vanilla extract

1 tub mascarpone

⅛ cup Kahlúa

⅛ cup Baileys Irish Cream

⅛ cup Tia Maria

Ladyfinger cookies (savoiardi)

PROCEDURE

Prepare espresso in water. Whisk powdered sugar and egg yolks to combine. Place over a pot with boiling water and continue to whisk until mixture reaches 140°F–150°F. Set aside to cool. Whisk granulated sugar, cream of tartar, and egg whites to stiff peaks. In a third bowl, whip heavy cream and vanilla paste or extract. Place mascarpone in large bowl. Gently fold in cooled egg mixture. Gently fold in egg whites. Gently fold in whipped cream. Keep mixture over ice. Add Kahlúa, Baileys, and Tia Maria to cooled espresso. Quickly dip ladyfingers in espresso mixture. Place in a single layer in a large rectangular glass baking dish. *(Tip: Layer cookies in the same direction for ease of cutting.)* Add a generous layer of the mascarpone mixture. Add another layer of dipped ladyfingers. Top with a generous layer of the mascarpone mixture. Cover and place in freezer.

TIP: *This recipe requires excellent timing. You must have all your ingredients and equipment in place before you begin. If any of your liquids separate, leave the more liquid parts out of your final cream.*

Chapter 4

ITALIAN SOUL FOOD

EVERYONE LOVES GOOD, OLD-FASHIONED home cooking. Every culture has its soul food, right? For Italian-Americans, the dishes are simple and from the heart. For me, there are some dishes that remind me of my mom's cooking; others are foods from my childhood that I couldn't get when I moved to Arizona; some are my mom's take on American classics; some are just delicious and remind you of someone, something, or someplace.

Making one of my favorite roasts.

Cooking with my children and their children is a family tradition.

As soon as you walked into my home as a child, Celeste would say, "What do you want to eat? What can I make you?" There were little things Mom and Dad would put together that were soul food. If there was nothing in the house—which was rare—Mom would

"Soul food has no boundaries. It can be few or many ingredients."

—Clara Lizio Melchiorre

whip up Pasta Piselli. Pasta with peas, so simple, so soulful: onion perfectly sautéed, frozen peas cooked till just green, and salt and pepper. Sprinkle some cheese for soul food perfection. At the restaurant at the end of a shift, we'd make a huge pot and everyone would take a break to eat. It tasted like heaven.

My brother Anthony reminded me of a funny story from when we were young. When the first fall moon was full, Pa would have Mom and the boys in our secret woods at daybreak. The boys carried full bushels of cauliflower and button mushrooms back through the cornfield to the car, following the same row or we'd be lost. Back and forth, back and forth, through the corn. It was worth it. Lunch was the best...pork chop and banana pepper or pepper and egg sandwiches. My mom would make gold with her sandwiches.

Then there's Zeppole di Baccala (salted dry cod that's been rehydrated)—these fritters are a classic for Christmas but delicious anytime. I think of them as soul food par excellence: flaky codfish fried in a fluffy batter. They're light and salty and comforting.

I hope that you are inspired by my soul food dishes to create your own.

ST. JOSEPH PASTRY
(a.k.a. Zeppole di San Giuseppe)

There's a famous Sicilian bakery in Chicago called Allegretti's. Hands down, they make the best St. Joseph's Day pastry, called Sfingi di San Giuseppe in Sicilian. It's basically a cream puff with an Italian pastry cream. I couldn't find any in Arizona, so I did my own take on it by tweaking a French pâte à choux dough by frying it like a doughnut. The secret: Drop the batter in oil and let it fry freely.

INGREDIENTS

For dough:

- 1 cup water
- ¾ stick butter
- 1⅛ tsp salt
- 1 Tbsp sugar
- 5¾ oz flour
- 1 cup eggs *(about 4 large eggs and 2 egg whites)*
- 3 cups olive oil for frying

For pastry cream:

- 1 cup milk
- 1½ cups heavy cream
- 3 egg yolks
- ⅓ cup sugar
- 1 pinch salt
- 2½ Tbsp flour
- 1 tsp vanilla extract

PROCEDURE

Make the dough: Boil water, butter, salt, and sugar. Add flour, whisk and remove from heat. After whisking well, return to heat until all flour is incorporated and dough forms a ball. Transfer to mixer. Let cool for 3–4 minutes. At low speed, add eggs one at a time. In a small pot with deep sides, heat oil to 325°F–350°F degrees. Once all eggs have been incorporated, place in a piping bag fitted with a round tip. Pipe golf ball–size shapes onto aluminum foil and drop into your heated oil with the foil. Remove foil with tongs. When golden on one side, turn. Remove from oil when browned and place on rack.

Make the pastry cream: Heat milk and cream. Separate yolks. Add sugar, salt, and flour; whisk together. Temper by adding a third of the heated milk and cream to the egg yolk mixture. Whisk together. Add tempered mixture to heated milk and whisk. Continuously whisk over medium to low heat. Bring to a boil and cook for an additional 2 minutes before removing. Add vanilla extract and use plastic wrap to cover the custard. Allow to cool.

Assembly: Add your cooled cream to a pastry bag and fill the zeppole. Slice your zeppole horizontally, fill with cream, and enjoy!

PEPPERS & EGGS SANDWICH

One of my mom's friends saw us one day and asked, "Celeste, can you make me peppers and eggs?" It has been a Lenten favorite from childhood, since you couldn't eat meat on Fridays during that time of year. We went back to the restaurant and made it. From that first batch of peppers and eggs, every Thursday after, we had to cut a bushel of peppers to make enough! At Celeste's, we had quite a few customers from the nearby Sears Roebuck.

INGREDIENTS

3 Tbsp extra-virgin olive oil

½ large onion, sliced

2 green bell peppers, seeded and sliced

7 large eggs

1 tsp sea salt

1 tsp freshly ground black pepper

Grated Pecorino cheese to taste

1 loaf Italian bread, toasted

PROCEDURE

Heat oil and add onion. Sauté until translucent. Add peppers. Cook about 7 minutes on medium heat. In a bowl, beat eggs, salt, and pepper. Add to pepper and onion mix. Using a wooden spoon, stir the eggs into the vegetable mixture. When eggs are cooked, remove from heat. Serve on warmed Italian bread.

PASTA & PEAS
(a.k.a. Pasta Piselli)

INGREDIENTS
- 1 lb mini shell pasta
- 3 large white onions, finely chopped
- ¼ cup olive oil
- 3 lbs frozen peas
- ½ cup olive oil
- ½ tsp salt
- ½ tsp pepper

PROCEDURE

In a large pot, sauté the chopped onions in ¼ cup olive oil until translucent. Add frozen peas, olive oil, salt, and pepper. *(Note: May appear to be too much oil. Remember, a little pasta water and oil are what will make better "sauce.")* Start cooking mini shell pasta in another large pot a few minutes after adding peas to onions. Drain mini shells and transfer them to peas and onions while they are still sautéing. Make sure shells are slightly uncooked before adding to peas and onions—they will finish cooking together.

CLARA'S BAGEL CHIPS

If you have some leftover bagels, you can slice them up, toast, and season to make a savory snack. The quantities really don't matter; you can kind of eyeball. You really do need a meat slicer to get the bagels thin enough.

EQUIPMENT
  1 home meat slicer
  4 half-size baking trays with Silpat cooking sheets
  3 deep full-size aluminum trays
  1 silicone pastry brush
  Safety gloves

INGREDIENTS
  12 one-day-old plain bagels
  Clara's garlic olive oil (page 20)
  Sea salt

PROCEDURE
Using safety gloves, slice bagels as thin as possible. Test-cut until you have a full-size bagel chip, because that will determine the size of the rest of your bagel chips. Begin slicing 1 side of the bagel as far as

Arizona Congressman Harry Mitchell would ask me to make my bagel chips for all his meet and greets!

you can, then turn over and slice as close as safely possible. Place all stacks of bagel chip slices on aluminum tray. Set aside any unsliced portion. On another full-size aluminum tray, place a bowl of garlic olive oil in corner. With a silicone pastry brush, begin to coat the top

of each bagel slice, then stack as you go.

To bake chips: Place a single line of bagel slices on 2 lined baking trays and sprinkle sea salt lightly over each slice. Place in preheated 375°F oven and bake until golden. Halfway through, turn the trays front to back. While the first trays are in the oven, prepare the other trays. When bagel chips are cooked, remove from oven and place on a paper towel–lined aluminum tray. Serve and enjoy—well worth all the effort!

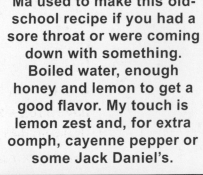

Mom's Home Remedy

Ma used to make this old-school recipe if you had a sore throat or were coming down with something. Boiled water, enough honey and lemon to get a good flavor. My touch is lemon zest and, for extra oomph, cayenne pepper or some Jack Daniel's.

GRAMMA CELESTE'S FRENCH TOAST

I remember the first time I went to a diner and ordered French toast. I was like, "What is this?" I was only used to my mom's, which was battered bread fried in oil.

INGREDIENTS

1 cup olive oil	1 Tbsp baking powder
9 slices of bread	2 Tbsp sugar
4 eggs	Pinch of salt
1 cup milk	Powdered sugar
1 cup flour	

PROCEDURE

Heat 1 cup olive oil over medium heat to 350°F in an 8-quart skillet with high sides. Cut crust off bread and into triangles. Combine wet ingredients in a bowl and dry ingredients in another bowl. Combine ingredients until mixture has the consistency of a liquid pancake batter. Dip the bread into the batter, turning over to make sure it is fully coated. Then fry the bread, 4 triangles at a time, in a skillet of heated oil until golden brown on each side. (The bread should be floating in the oil. You will need to scrape it from the bottom if it gets stuck.) Take bread out of oil and place on a plate lined with paper towels to drain. Place on serving platter and sprinkle with powdered sugar. Serve with pure maple syrup or your favorite topping.

CHILI CELESTE

My mom just made a great chili...and I am happy to share the recipe with you.

INGREDIENTS

 1 lb ground turkey

 1 lb ground chicken

 1 cup chopped onions

 1 large garlic clove

 1 Tbsp salt

 ½ Tbsp pepper

 2 Tbsp chili powder

 Olive oil

 1 28-oz can San Marzano tomatoes

 2 15-oz cans red kidney beans

 4 adobo chilies (from can)

PROCEDURE

Combine ground turkey, ground chicken, chopped onions, garlic, salt, pepper, and chili powder. Sauté in olive oil and stir. Add San Marzano tomatoes, hand-crushed. Add both cans of red kidney beans. Add the adobo chilies. Allow to simmer.

Never use too much sauce, it makes the pizza soggy.

Keep sauce and toppings clear of outer crust.

A beautiful veggie pizza by my son Rudy.

Assemble the pizza: Brush a little garlic olive oil on the circular dough to prevent it from absorbing the tomatoes and weakening the dough. Ladle enough sauce to cover the dough, leaving about an inch all around for the crust. Don't over-sauce your pizza, or it will come out soggy. Add a layer of your choice of toppings, then finish with a layer of shredded mozzarella.

ADDING TOPPINGS: *Always place toppings on top of the sauce—not the cheese. This way, the flavor will blend into and enrich the sauce.*

Fried Dough Deliciousness

A favorite of mine that my parents made was fried pizza dough, savory or sweet. Take a piece of the dough, stretch it into little pieces, and fry it on the stove. Turn once. You can make it savory by sprinkling salt on it while warm or sweet by sprinkling granulated sugar. It's delicious either way.

Everyone Loves MEATBALLS

INGREDIENTS

- 2½ lbs ground beef
- 2½ lbs ground pork
- 1 Tbsp black pepper
- 1½ Tbsp sea salt
- 3 cups Romano cheese
- ½ cup fresh basil, chopped
- ½ cup fresh parsley, chopped
- 2 cups milk-soaked bread; remove excess milk and crumble
- 6 eggs

My right hands at Clara's.

PROCEDURE

Combine all ingredients except eggs in a large mixing bowl. Mix ingredients together with your hands. Beat eggs in a separate bowl. Add to the meat mixture in 3 parts. With each egg addition, blend into the meat mixture well before adding the next egg addition. Test the meat mixture seasoning by frying a small amount. Adjust seasoning before the next step. Roll into balls and place on baking sheet brushed with olive oil. Bake at 400°F until browned. *(Tip: Time varies based on size of meatball; 1-inch meatballs cook in about 30 minutes.)* You can make the mixture a day before and store in a zip-top bag. Use an ice cream scoop to remove meat with ease.

MAKE THEM GLUTEN-FREE: For a no-carb or gluten-free meatball, substitute Italian bread with a loaf of gluten-free bread *or* 1 pound of shredded mozzarella.

TRY IT WITH POULTRY: To make with a combination of turkey and chicken meat, add a pound of grated mozzarella to meat mixture.

PORK CHOPS & VINEGAR PEPPERS

INGREDIENTS

1½ lbs red potatoes

1½ lbs thin pork chops, bone-in or bone-out *(bone-in preferred)*

4 Tbsp garlic olive oil (page 20)

Olive oil for pan

Salt and pepper to taste

1½ cups vinegar peppers, mild or hot *(You can use ours, page 28, or store-bought banana pepper rings in vinegar.)*

¼ cup vinegar juice *(brine from the jar)*

PROCEDURE

Jump-start your potatoes: Preheat oven to 400°F. Slice potatoes into ⅛-inch-thick rounds. On a baking sheet, place potatoes; toss with garlic oil, salt, and pepper. Bake until the potatoes are almost done, about 20 minutes, turning occasionally. While they're in the oven, prepare your pork. Pat meat dry, then salt and pepper both sides. In a large sauté pan on medium-high heat, add olive oil just to coat the bottom of the pan lightly. Fry both sides, just enough to brown a little. When chops are almost done, add peppers to the pan to get them started cooking. Transfer pork and peppers to casserole dish. Arrange potatoes on top, then pour vinegar juice over the top. Place back in oven and bake until potatoes are slightly crisp and the pork registers at 150°F, about 10 minutes.

TIP: *You can keep covered in foil, in the oven, until you are ready to serve.*

BEEF BROTH
(The Original Bone Broth)

INGREDIENTS

2 lbs beef shank

5 lbs beef chuck

4 lbs beef bone marrow bones

1 gallon cold water

1 large yellow onion

2 bay leaves

1 28-oz can San Marzano tomatoes

1 Tbsp whole peppercorns

3 Tbsp sea salt

1 lb celery

1 lb carrots

Freezer soup bag: Peelings from carrots, celery, and onions

Parsley stems

PROCEDURE

Preheat oven to 400°F. Place marrow bones on a half-sheet pan fitted with a wire rack. Place bones in oven and roast for at least 1 hour or until all fat has rendered. Fill a 14-quart heavy-bottomed pot with 1 gallon cold water. Add beef shank, beef chuck, and beef bones to pot set on high heat. As soup heats up and comes to a boil, skim off any foam release. While soup is coming to a boil, prepare other ingredients: Wash and quarter unpeeled onion, then put in bowl; peel carrots and celery, then cut off top and bottom and set aside middle pieces. (The tops, bottoms, and peelings go in the bowl with the quartered onions; combine all in a freezer bag to use later.) Pour San Marzano tomatoes in bowl, then chop or crush by hand. Once soup has come to full boil, add onions, carrots, celery, bay leaves, tomatoes, 2 tablespoons salt, 1 tablespoon whole peppercorns, parsley stems, and contents of freezer soup bag. Once all ingredients are added, allow soup to boil for an additional

Beef Salad with Onion Slices in Vinegar & Oil

As a special Monday night dinner, Mom and Dad would make the beef broth and serve a hearty bowl of soup. I would always say to Mom and Dad that the soup was only the first course—where is the main dish? Then they would transform the boiled beef into this simple but outstanding salad. This easy beef soup meat salad with thinly sliced onions was, and still is today, simply delicious!

PROCEDURE Cut beef into small bite-size pieces. Slice onion into very thin slices. Add salt and black pepper. Add vinegar and olive oil. Toss and serve. You can also add a hearty lettuce like romaine.

10 minutes. Reduce heat to a low boil and cook for an hour and a half, or as much as needed. Taste soup for seasoning; if needed, add an additional tablespoon of salt. Turn off heat and cover. Allow soup to cool down, then remove bay leaves and strain meat and veggies from broth. Using a fat separator, further strain any excess fat or particles from broth. This beef broth can be used for a variety of different dishes, such as beef vegetable soup, beef barley soup, and beef stew, as well as a base for any of your favorite beef soup applications. Unused broth can be frozen for future use.

Chapter 5

MY FAMILY'S FAVORITE DISHES

With my beautiful children.

"These hands will feed the world."

—*Teresina, Mama Celeste Lizio's mom*

WHEN MY MOM, CELESTE, left her small town in southern Italy, she was already known as an inspired cook. Her mother, Teresina, sent her off to America with a small ambition—to feed the world. Well, as you know, my mom did come close, with millions of pizzas sold under her Mama Celeste Lizio brand.

Food for the Lizios and Melchiorres has always meant family. Any meal at our home usually starts with a conversation on what our next meal will be. Cooking is my whole life. When I married Rudolph, two strong Italian cooking factions came together.

I'll never forget when Rudy surprised his mom, Elsie, and his Aunt Polonia with me for dinner. When I walked in, they were already eating at the table and Rudy presented me. It was Saturday evening, and there was definitely enough food. Every Saturday, Aunt Polonia would do shopping for two to three hours, even though dinner was always the same: sirloin steak salad, broccoli soup, and Ersilia's Potatoes Rosemary. No matter how many she made, there were never enough potatoes. Truly, food of the gods, ambrosia. In this chapter, I have selected the dishes most requested by my family.

Rudy and me on our wedding day.

With my love, Rudy.

Enjoying a night out with my brother-in-law John
and my brother Tony ("Uncle T").

Savoring flavors with my son Mark.

Touring Italy with my brother Will and his wife, Marilyn.

With my friend Marilyn and two of my beautiful daughters-in-law, Andrea and Erika.

"For me, family is everything."

—Clara Lizio Melchiorre

Cooking with my granddaughter.

With Michelle and my brother-in-law John in Arizona.

ANTIPASTO, CLARA-STYLE

Can an Italian meal possibly start without antipasto? Antipasto was often so abbondante *at our house that new friends wouldn't realize there was more to come after the cold cuts!*

INGREDIENTS

Prosciutto: *Manny at Mia Famiglia was the best prosciutto slicer this side of Italy! Four pieces per layer on paper. It was thin and delicious. I'd go there for cold cuts and mascarpone.*

Soppressata (hot or sweet)

Mortadella with pistachio, from Italy

Sharp Provolone cheese: *This was Mom and Dad's favorite. I shave it with a potato peeler, slice it thin, and roll it into sliced mortadella, or serve it cubed.*

Cubed Fontinella cheese

Bread on the side

You should throw something in for color. Speaking of "adding color," I used to get in trouble at the restaurant for adding black olives to the house salad to brighten it up. Rudy Jr. had the dishwasher count how many people actually ate the olives. It was very few, and adding the olives was costing us thousands of dollars a year. Even when restaurants are doing well, you always have to keep an eye on the finances. In this case, though, I didn't give in to commerce and stuck with my artistic approach to salad.

GRAMMA ERSILIA'S POTATOES ROSEMARY

Getting Gramma Ersilia's (she became "Elsie" in America) recipes wasn't always easy. She kept her secrets well guarded. Eventually—let's not talk about how—I was able to get a few. This one is my favorite.

INGREDIENTS

- **4 whole potatoes, cut into full-length wedges with skin on**
- **2 Tbsp olive oil**
- **2 Tbsp rosemary, roughly chopped**
- **1 Tbsp smashed whole garlic or garlic oil** *(I use garlic purée)*
- **¼ tsp salt**
- **¼ tsp pepper**

PROCEDURE

Preheat oven to 400°F. In large mixing bowl, add potato wedges. Toss in olive oil, then add the remaining seasonings. Add potatoes to baking sheet. Cook 30–40 minutes, tossing occasionally until crispy on the outside but soft on the inside. Broil for a short time to make them extra crispy.

TIP: *Sprinkle extra olive oil on the potatoes before roasting—that was Elsie's trick!*

NOTE: *These potatoes are not the same as the ones used in my Chicken Vesuvio (page 72).*

Rosemary Potatoes with Chicken

Prep your chicken parts with garlic olive oil (page 20), then add salt, pepper, and rosemary. Toss in a bowl. Place on a baking sheet with the potatoes and roast together.

BROCCOLI RABE WITH GARLIC
(a.k.a. Rapini)

This is one of my favorite easy recipes. You can prep your vegetables (see below) and then sauté when ready. Add anchovies for extra kick—that's how my son Mark and daughter-in-law Erika like them. And reheat with some cannellini beans (from your cupboard) for a Day 2 meal.

HOW TO PREP BROCCOLI RABE

1. Cut the bottom ½ inch off the stems.

2. Separate into leaves, stems, and florets under running water.

3. When done, cut the stems into small pieces. Cut leaves into 2–3 pieces so they are bite-size.

4. Wrap leaves, stems, and florets separately in paper towels and store in a zip-top bag.

5. This can be done 2–3 days before you need it.

INGREDIENTS

- Bunch of broccoli rabe, cleaned and prepped
- 1 2-oz can of Cento-brand flat anchovies, cut into 3 or 4 segments
- 3 Tbsp olive oil
- 3 garlic cloves, sliced thin
- Chicken broth (optional)
- Salt and pepper to taste

PROCEDURE

Sauté garlic in olive oil in a pan large enough to hold the rapini and add your anchovies. Before it gets brown and starts dancing, add stems. Cook for 2 minutes. Then push it to the side of the pan. Add florets. Use tongs and start to incorporate them into the stems. Add a smidgen of salt. Add leaves. Reduce heat to a simmer. Cover. Add a little chicken broth, if needed, but usually the moisture from the greens will be enough. Add black pepper to taste. Cook until it wilts down.

STEAK 'LA MODE
(a.k.a. Steak Toto)

Credit where it's due. This is my brother Anthony's (I started calling him Toto more than a few years ago) recipe. He got it from my dad, but has made it his specialty. He makes it every Christmas Day, and the whole family looks forward to eating it.

INGREDIENTS

- 4 rib eye steaks, 1½-inch thick, some of the fat removed
- ½ tsp salt
- ½ tsp pepper
- ½ oz flour
- ½ oz olive oil
- 1 oz butter
- 2 cups onion, sliced

- 1 lb portobello mushrooms, sliced
- 2 leeks, sliced
- ½ oz garlic emulsion (page 20)
- ¼ cup sherry wine
- 1 cup beef broth
- 1 Tbsp parsley, chopped
- 1 Tbsp basil, torn
- Red pepper flakes (optional)

PROCEDURE

Salt and pepper each side of steaks. Dredge in flour. In a frying pan over medium flame, heat olive oil and butter, add steaks and brown on both sides. Set in a single layer in baking pan. Add onion, portobello mushrooms, and leeks to frying pan; sauté until tender and crisp, then add the garlic and sherry wine. Sizzle until wine is spent. In a stockpot, boil the beef broth. Add veggie mix, parsley, basil, salt, pepper, and, if using, red pepper flakes for just a little kick. Simmer and thicken. Spoon veggie mix generously over steaks (not too much broth or the meat will boil). Bake at 350°F until meat is really tender, about 20 minutes.

Clara's Take on
STEAK FIORENTINA

INGREDIENTS (FOR EACH STEAK)

- 1 3-inch-thick porterhouse steak
- 1 Tbsp garlic olive oil purée (page 20)
- 1 Tbsp rosemary, chopped
- 1 Tbsp olive oil
- Salt and pepper
- 1 Tbsp butter

PROCEDURE

Place steaks on a baking tray. Rub garlic purée on top and bottom of each steak. Sprinkle with salt and pepper. Cover in plastic wrap. Let sit about an hour at room temperature. Heat 1 tablespoon olive oil in a heavy-bottomed, oven-safe pan. Sear the steaks about 5–8 minutes on each side over medium-high heat. Then place in a broiler on high heat, on the highest rack, for about 3 minutes. When done, remove from oven, sprinkle with rosemary, and place a tablespoon of butter on top. Tent the meat to let it rest.

OPTIONS: *I'm a purist. I like my steak as steak. I have this battle all the time with the kids. You can season the butter with any herb or flavored salt you like. My son Mark loves truffle salt.*

1-2-3 Steak (a.k.a. Jake's Steak)

The secret to my grandson's favorite is getting your rib eye steaks cut ⅛th of an inch. This is great for a last-minute dinner because you can season and freeze the raw meat to pull out of the freezer any time.

INGREDIENTS

- ⅓ cup garlic olive oil
- 1 lb boneless rib eye, cut ⅛-inch thick
- Salt and pepper, to taste
- Optional: Hot Pepper Oil (page 22)

PROCEDURE

Season meat by rubbing garlic olive oil on it. Heat up a cast-iron pan. Sear the Steak 1-2-3 on one side until brown; turn and repeat for the other side. Season with salt and pepper. Add a little hot pepper oil for heat. Serve with toasted ciabatta bread or sliced peasant bread.

THE ONLY LAMB MARINADE YOU NEED

This marinade reminds me of a funny story. I'll never forget the time that my friend Roseanne took Anthony and Michelle home after school for me because I had to take Ma to something in the city. Roseanne asked Michelle, who was in third grade at the time, what she'd like for lunch. "Lamb chops would be fine," Michelle replied politely. Roseanne later told me, "I can't get peanut butter and jelly down Laura's mouth." You can use this marinade on any cut—I use it on chops or legs.

INGREDIENTS

Zest of 2 large lemons

Juice from lemons (about ½ cup)

2 Tbsp salt

1 Tbsp black pepper, coarsely ground

2 Tbsp oregano, preferably dry
(Measure amount needed, then rub between hands for a release of incredible aroma.)

1 Tbsp fresh rosemary, coarsely chopped

¾ cup olive oil

½ cup fresh parsley, coarsely chopped and firmly packed in a cup

Leg of lamb or any cut of lamb chop
(I like the shoulder chops.)

PROCEDURE

Make the marinade: Take all ingredients except lamb and pulse in a food processor. Put lamb in marinade. Refrigerate up to 2 hours, turning occasionally to cover all the meat. Remove from fridge a half hour before you are ready to grill.

Cook the lamb: Turn the grill on high heat. When grill is ready, use a paper towel and fold it into a small packet. With long tongs, dip it in oil and coat grill rack. Turn heat down to low. Remove lamb from marinade, shaking off excess, and place on grill. At time of cooking, salt and pepper lamb before putting on grill. Caution: Drippings from the marinade will cause the fire to flare up! Not to worry—just move the lamb, but do not turn the meat over. Allow it to get a nice char before turning. Turn off 1 end burner. Turn lamb over and place on the 2 open burners and continue to grill. Place marinade in a baking tray, put over the closed burner, and close lid. Cook to your desired temperature. At the end, give it a good salt and pepper. Place lamb on the tray with marinade. Allow to rest and then enjoy.

Clara's Take on
STEAK FIORENTINA

INGREDIENTS (FOR EACH STEAK)

- 1 3-inch-thick porterhouse steak
- 1 Tbsp garlic olive oil purée (page 20)
- 1 Tbsp rosemary, chopped
- 1 Tbsp olive oil
- Salt and pepper
- 1 Tbsp butter

PROCEDURE

Place steaks on a baking tray. Rub garlic purée on top and bottom of each steak. Sprinkle with salt and pepper. Cover in plastic wrap. Let sit about an hour at room temperature. Heat 1 tablespoon olive oil in a heavy-bottomed, oven-safe pan. Sear the steaks about 5–8 minutes on each side over medium-high heat. Then place in a broiler on high heat, on the highest rack, for about 3 minutes. When done, remove from oven, sprinkle with rosemary, and place a tablespoon of butter on top. Tent the meat to let it rest.

OPTIONS: *I'm a purist. I like my steak as steak. I have this battle all the time with the kids. You can season the butter with any herb or flavored salt you like. My son Mark loves truffle salt.*

1-2-3 Steak (a.k.a. Jake's Steak)

The secret to my grandson's favorite is getting your rib eye steaks cut ⅛th of an inch. This is great for a last-minute dinner because you can season and freeze the raw meat to pull out of the freezer any time.

INGREDIENTS

- ⅓ cup garlic olive oil
- 1 lb boneless rib eye, cut ⅛-inch thick
- Salt and pepper, to taste
- Optional: Hot Pepper Oil (page 22)

PROCEDURE

Season meat by rubbing garlic olive oil on it. Heat up a cast-iron pan. Sear the Steak 1-2-3 on one side until brown; turn and repeat for the other side. Season with salt and pepper. Add a little hot pepper oil for heat. Serve with toasted ciabatta bread or sliced peasant bread.

THE ONLY LAMB MARINADE YOU NEED

This marinade reminds me of a funny story. I'll never forget the time that my friend Roseanne took Anthony and Michelle home after school for me because I had to take Ma to something in the city. Roseanne asked Michelle, who was in third grade at the time, what she'd like for lunch. "Lamb chops would be fine," Michelle replied politely. Roseanne later told me, "I can't get peanut butter and jelly down Laura's mouth." You can use this marinade on any cut—I use it on chops or legs.

INGREDIENTS

Zest of 2 large lemons

Juice from lemons (about ½ cup)

2 Tbsp salt

1 Tbsp black pepper, coarsely ground

2 Tbsp oregano, preferably dry
(Measure amount needed, then rub between hands for a release of incredible aroma.)

1 Tbsp fresh rosemary, coarsely chopped

¾ cup olive oil

½ cup fresh parsley, coarsely chopped and firmly packed in a cup

Leg of lamb or any cut of lamb chop
(I like the shoulder chops.)

PROCEDURE

Make the marinade: Take all ingredients except lamb and pulse in a food processor. Put lamb in marinade. Refrigerate up to 2 hours, turning occasionally to cover all the meat. Remove from fridge a half hour before you are ready to grill.

Cook the lamb: Turn the grill on high heat. When grill is ready, use a paper towel and fold it into a small packet. With long tongs, dip it in oil and coat grill rack. Turn heat down to low. Remove lamb from marinade, shaking off excess, and place on grill. At time of cooking, salt and pepper lamb before putting on grill. Caution: Drippings from the marinade will cause the fire to flare up! Not to worry—just move the lamb, but do not turn the meat over. Allow it to get a nice char before turning. Turn off 1 end burner. Turn lamb over and place on the 2 open burners and continue to grill. Place marinade in a baking tray, put over the closed burner, and close lid. Cook to your desired temperature. At the end, give it a good salt and pepper. Place lamb on the tray with marinade. Allow to rest and then enjoy.

WORKS WELL WITH CHICKEN, TOO! *Marinate your chicken, then reduce the extra marinade with a pat of butter to make a wonderful sauce to serve with your cooked chicken. Pass sauce through a fine strainer before serving.*

SLOW-COOKED BEEF STEW

We used to make this for my son Anthony's office. They just loved this hearty lunch. It was one of their favorites.

INGREDIENTS

- 5 lbs boneless beef short ribs
- 2 cups unbleached flour
- 1 Tbsp sea salt
- 2 tsp coarse black pepper
- ¼ cup pure olive oil
- 1 large yellow onion
- 1 lb celery
- 1 lb carrots
- 3 lbs red potatoes
- 2 lbs mushrooms (1 lb baby bella, 1 lb white)
- 3 Tbsp garlic olive oil (page 20)
- 1 28-oz can San Marzano tomatoes
- 4 large garlic cloves
- 1 cup dry red wine
- 2 quarts beef broth
- ¼ oz fresh basil
- ¼ cup flat Italian parsley
- 1½ Tbsp cornstarch
- 2 large, deep aluminum cooking trays, stacked

PROCEDURE

Preheat oven to 400°F. Combine flour, salt, and pepper in a large bowl. Cut each beef short rib into 3 or 4 diagonal pieces and season with salt, pepper, and garlic olive oil; set aside. To prepare veggies: Cut onion root to stem in half; cut off top and peel onion but keep root intact. Then cut onion into quarter-inch slices, and set aside peel and root in a freezer soup bag for later use. (Also save the peelings and trimmings of the carrots and celery in bag.) Peel and cut carrots and celery into diagonal 1½-inch pieces; set aside. Wipe mushrooms, then cut into quarters. Peel potatoes, then cut each in half, then cut each half into smaller pieces. Add all chopped veggies to the doubled deep aluminum tray and toss with garlic olive oil, salt, and pepper, then cook in preheated oven for 20 minutes. Put garlic cloves in a food processor and finely chop. Pour can of tomatoes in a bowl and crush by hand. Add ¼ cup of olive oil to a large, heavy-bottomed cooking pot set over medium-high heat. Flour the

beef and shake off excess with strainer and sear meat in a single layer for 4–5 minutes on each side, then set aside (it will take a couple of batches). Add chopped garlic to pot and stir, then immediately add 1 cup of dry red wine and begin to deglaze bottom of pot. Add 6 cups of beef broth and bring to a boil. With remaining 2 cups of beef broth, add 1½ tablespoons of cornstarch and stir well to blend; set aside. Taste beef broth for seasoning; add additional salt and pepper if needed. Once broth has come to a boil, add cold beef broth and cornstarch mixture to pot and stir well. Remove roasted veggies from oven, then add the beef, beef broth, parsley, basil, and crushed tomatoes, and gently mix together. Cover tray with foil, then cook in oven for 1 hour. After 30 minutes, turn tray halfway. After 1 hour, remove foil cover and stir gently; cook in oven uncovered for an extra 15–20 minutes.

Holiday Cooking

BACK IN MY RESTAURANT YEARS, we often spent holidays at the restaurant. More recently, we have all been together in our homes. Last Christmas was the first one where I passed the wooden spoon to my daughter-in-law Erika. She is the keeper of the Feast of the 7 Fishes.

Rudy's family and I celebrating Turkey Day at Clara's.

THANKSGIVING

In our house, the turkey legs were at a premium. There used to be strikes by those who did not get the leg (Rudy Sr. and Jr.)! Thank goodness extra turkey legs are now more readily available. I remember when I was growing up, my dad, Anthony, miraculously created four legs out of the two wings as well.

When we opened up Clara's, a new holiday tradition was born. We put all our restaurant tables together in a big square and invited in all who needed a place to celebrate. One favorite memory is Rudy Jr.'s friend Chris Cobb, who would almost punctually appear at 9:25 p.m.—he would have his family dinner and then make his way over to us! We would all look to the parking lot for Chris and his warm smile and big appetite!

GRAMMA CELESTE'S TURKEY STUFFING

This was my mother's turkey dressing recipe. For as long as I can remember, dressing for me was a meatloaf-type dish. Imagine my surprise when I first saw a "traditional" dressing! I have watched this recipe travel down and out of the family tree, from my family to yours. Thanksgiving is truly one of my favorite holidays and always is an intricate mix of family traditions. My mother, Celeste, had

a favorite stuffing that was uniquely hers. It is more of a spicy, garlicky meatloaf than a dressing and was made separately from the turkey. My mother-in-law, Ersilia, had a giblet, nutmeg, and rice-based dressing that had the most wonderful smell and taste.

INGREDIENTS

- 1 large leek (white part, sliced medium-thin)
- 1 medium onion, coarsely chopped
- 1 large celery stalk with leaves, peeled and coarsely chopped
- 3 lbs ground chuck
- 1 lb ground pork
- ½ Tbsp sea salt
- 1 tsp coarsely ground black pepper
- 4 large garlic cloves, finely chopped
- 1 lb dry bread, soaked in milk; squeeze well, then add to meat
- 8 large eggs, slightly beaten
- 2 cups Pecorino Romano cheese

- 1 bunch flat-leaf parsley, leaves only
- 1 packet fresh basil, leaves only, julienne cut
- 10 sage leaves or 1 packet, leaves only, julienne cut
- ½ Tbsp sea salt
- 1 tsp coarsely ground black pepper
- 1 Tbsp poultry seasoning
- 4–5 cups turkey or chicken stock
- 1 lb Italian artisan bread or Old World bread, ½-inch slice, cut into large cubes *(Place in bowl, toss with garlic oil. Add Parmigiano-Reggiano cheese, place on baking sheet and toast in oven until golden and crisp. Cool, then add to stuffing mixture just before baking so they don't get soggy.)*

Holiday Cooking

This is me enjoying one of my granddaughter Jackie's desserts. She would personally deliver them to me.

PROCEDURE

Preheat oven to 400°F. Measure and prepare all ingredients. Place ground chuck and pork in large mixing bowl (large enough to accommodate all ingredients). Add sea salt, black pepper, squeezed bread, and garlic and mix well by hand. Add beaten eggs; mix. Add Pecorino Romano cheese; mix. Add leek, onion, celery, parsley, basil, sage, poultry seasoning, remaining sea salt, and black pepper; mix.

NOTE: When ready to bake, add cooled toasted garlic bread cubes to meat mixture. Mix well to incorporate all ingredients, but you should still be able to see the toasted bread cubes.

TO BAKE:

Use a large baking pan, ½-size baking sheet pan, or table-size aluminum steam tray (doubled for stability). Lightly coat tray with olive oil spray. Form two parallel logs of the dressing mixture in pan. Add 3 or 4 cups of turkey or chicken stock to pan. Cover with aluminum foil and place in 400°F oven for 20 minutes. Remove foil, baste, add additional stock if needed, cover again with foil, and rotate pan. Bake another 20 minutes. Remove foil, baste, and bake till dressing is beautifully roasted, 5–10 minutes. Remove from oven, cover with foil until you are ready to serve.

NOTE: I prepare my dressing the night before. After I have mixed all ingredients, I place my dressing in 2 large zip-top bags overnight in the refrigerator so all the seasonings blend together. Thanksgiving morning I bake my dressing and then the turkey.

TURKEY SHEPHERD'S PIE

This is a great way to get rid of all your Thanksgiving leftovers.

LAYERS OF:
- Chopped turkey
- Green beans
- Stuffing
- Sweet and white potatoes
- Broccoli/cauliflower
- Gravy
- Mashed potatoes
- Black pepper

PROCEDURE
Bake at 375°F for 45 minutes.

TURKEY DINNER ON A BUN
(a.k.a. Mark's After-Thanksgiving Sandwich)

This is a sandwich my son likes to make—and another way to get rid of the extras.

INGREDIENTS
- Thanksgiving leftovers
  (We use turkey, gravy, rapini, cranberry sauce.)
- Vinegar peppers, page 28
- Loaf of Italian bread

PROCEDURE
Start by slicing open your bread. Layer turkey, gravy, rapini, hot peppers, and cranberry sauce, and then toast in the oven until warm and the bread is crispy.

Holiday Cooking

FRIED CALAMARI

My daughter-in-law Erika had to do a calamari practice run her first Christmas cooking. She and her daughter Ali came over. I gave specific instructions. She had to buy the right calamari, fresh and large. They dredged, they fried, under my watchful eye. They did great. We had to make sure the calamari weren't too chewy or overcooked.

INGREDIENTS

2 lbs high-quality calamari (squid), cleaned, washed and dried

> **TIP:** *When buying calamari, look for fish that is white and slightly translucent. The squid should be intact and uniform, with no patches of iridescence. The skin should be elastic but firm and not slimy.*

1 cup flour

Salt and pepper to taste

Olive oil for frying

PROCEDURE

Cut calamari into rings, leaving tentacles whole. Season flour with salt and pepper. Move the calamari through the flour and shake off excess before frying. Fry until golden in 325°F–350°F olive oil (see page 30 for my olive oil frying secret). Don't overstuff the fryer. The calamari should move freely. When 1 side is golden, use a slotted spoon to turn. Fry until other side is golden. Remove from oil and dry on paper towels. Sprinkle with salt while warm.

TIP: *Test your oil temperature by sprinkling flour in. If it immediately activates, the oil is ready. If it just sits on top, it's not.*

Holiday Cooking

PASTIERI

This is a favorite during the Lenten season, when Catholics can't eat meat on Fridays.

INGREDIENTS

- 1 lb perciatelli or spaghetti, cooked to package directions
- 2 eggs
- 1 lb ricotta filling (page 55)
- 2 Tbsp olive oil

PROCEDURE

Set oven to 400°F. Place baking pan with olive oil in the oven to heat while preparing Pastieri filling. Add the pasta and eggs to the ricotta and mix well. Pour into the heated oil. Bake for 30 minutes and remove from oven. Turn over Pastieri, replace in pan, and return to oven. Remove from oven when it is brown and crispy.

Holiday Cooking

AUNT MARILYN'S
(Soon-to-Be-Famous)
LEMON KNOT COOKIES

My granddaughter Jessica had tasted these cookies years ago when we made them in Arizona. She kept asking me each time I saw her when I was going to make her more lemon cookies! What is a grandma to do? I made her a batch and sent some photos to her dad. The next morning I received a call from Jessica—she had heard I made her cookies. She called to tell me she was on her way over to get them! I hope you enjoy Jessica's cookies as much as she does.

INGREDIENTS

7 oz melted butter

1 oz corn syrup

1 oz lemon extract

8 oz sugar

5 whole eggs

1½ lbs bread flour

1½ oz baking powder

For icing:

2 lbs powdered sugar

2 oz corn syrup

4½ oz hot water

1 tsp lemon extract

Dash of salt

PROCEDURE

Preheat oven to 400°F. Put paddle attachment on stand mixer, add melted butter, corn syrup, lemon extract, and sugar; blend. Add eggs to wet mixture. Then add dry ingredients (flour and baking powder). The mixture will be wet and sticky. Add ¼ cup more flour at a time as needed; we usually need an additional ½ cup. It is critical to make sure the dough is neither too sticky nor too dry. Test dough by flouring your hand and rolling a bit between your fingers while trying to form the knot. Stretch the dough; it should be elastic. Form dough into a square and let rest for a short time.

imparted to her through her mother, the famed Mama Celeste Lizio. Clara took her mother's cooking, respectfully, to another level.

Despite having no formal training, Clara was a student of the cooking game who spent the times she wasn't in the kitchen watching cooking shows or reading cookbooks. Even in retirement, and well into her final years, she loved and felt blessed to be able to take cooking classes run by top chefs in New York and Italy. On her last trip to Italy, she had to make a pilgrimage to see Franco Pepe's famous pizzeria, outside Naples. She adored more contemporary legends, such as Missy Robbins, whose cooking she found exceptional.

While much of this book is composed of family favorites and staple dishes from Clara's restaurant, Clara included her tips and tricks to perfect and improve upon easy side dishes up to sophisticated entrées. Clara could perfect any dish, from a peanut butter and jelly sandwich to a complex soufflé. All you had to do was tell her what you wanted, and she would find a way to make it hers—and mouthwatering to the last bite. By the end of her life, Clara had reached the status of a true culinary artist whose skills in the kitchen aged like a good bottle of wine, getting better year after year. The last pot of gravy she made may very well have been her best.

During her retirement, she would auction off a "Cooking with Clara" night. The event included a cooking class and full-course meal, followed by treasured stories being told over drinks and desserts. And, of course, the usual $5,000-plus proceeds from the auction all went to charity. As anyone who attended could attest, they were extraordinary moments, as she was in the masterful prime of her lifetime of culinary experience.

This book, just like every meal she cooked, was made with love. We hope with this book you will be able to celebrate the life of our beloved Clara and get to experience through her recipes the woman whose light will continue to shine inside all who are lucky enough to have known and loved her.

—Mark Melchiorre

Dear Mom,

Farewell notes from Clara's other three children.

"Mom, I feel so proud to take a page from your book. You, like your mom, knew it was never too late to do what you want. You both found great success in your 50s! You never worried about other people's timetables. You taught me not to leave a day on the table. You never stopped until you were done. You left this world on your own terms—and finished this book before you left. I love you, Mom. I miss you every day."

—Michelle Melchiorre

"My favorite childhood memories are seeing my mother and Grandma Celeste making dinner for our family."

—Anthony Melchiorre

"Clara's approach to cooking was like her approach to life. It doesn't matter the ingredients given to you, it's all about the love and joy you put into the process. And in the end, it's always about family."

—Rudy Melchiorre

RECIPE INDEX

CONVERSION CHARTS

METRIC AND IMPERIAL CONVERSIONS
(These conversions are rounded for convenience)

Ingredient	Cups/Table-spoons/ Teaspoons	Ounces	Grams/Milliliters
Butter	1 cup/ 16 tablespoons/ 2 sticks	8 ounces	230 grams
Cheese, shredded	1 cup	4 ounces	110 grams
Cream cheese	1 tablespoon	0.5 ounce	14.5 grams
Cornstarch	1 tablespoon	0.3 ounce	8 grams
Flour, all-purpose	1 cup/1 table-spoon	4.5 ounces/0.3 ounce	125 grams/ 8 grams
Flour, whole wheat	1 cup	4 ounces	120 grams
Fruit, dried	1 cup	4 ounces	120 grams
Fruits or veggies, chopped	1 cup	5 to 7 ounces	145 to 200 grams
Fruits or veggies, puréed	1 cup	8.5 ounces	245 grams
Honey, maple syrup, or corn syrup	1 tablespoon	0.75 ounce	20 grams
Liquids: cream, milk, water, or juice	1 cup	8 fluid ounces	240 milliliters
Oats	1 cup	5.5 ounces	150 grams
Salt	1 teaspoon	0.2 ounce	6 grams
Spices: cinnamon, cloves, ginger, or nutmeg (ground)	1 teaspoon	0.2 ounce	5 milliliters
Sugar, brown, firmly packed	1 cup	7 ounces	200 grams
Sugar, white	1 cup/1 table-spoon	7 ounces/0.5 ounce	200 grams/12.5 grams
Vanilla extract	1 teaspoon	0.2 ounce	4 grams

OVEN TEMPERATURES

Fahrenheit	Celsius	Gas Mark
225°	110°	¼
250°	120°	½
275°	140°	1
300°	150°	2
325°	160°	3
350°	180°	4
375°	190°	5
400°	200°	6
425°	220°	7
450°	230°	8